Mountain Moments

Photographs by Warren Brunner

Reflections by Al Fritsch, SJ

Acclaim Press

MORLEY, MISSOURI

Acclaim Press
— Your Next Great Book —

P.O. Box 238
Morley, Missouri 63767
(573) 472-9800
www.acclaimpress.com

Library of Congress Control Number: 2010924221

ISBN-13: 978-1-935001-42-3
ISBN-10: 1-935001-42-6

First Printing 2010
Printed in China
10 9 8 7 6 5 4 3 2 1

What others are saying about Warren Brunner and his photographs:

"All lovers of the Appalachian region and its people should have a copy of this book. Warren Brunner's splendid and timeless photographs and Al Fritsch's insightful reflections on the land and people and his scriptural references and prayers will heighten our awareness of the beauty and worth of this place and people and inspire us to do more to correct mistakes of the past and assure a bright future."
    – Loyal Jones
    Retired Director of the Berea College Appalachian Center

"Warren Brunner … helped Appalachia _see_ and _remember_ itself."
    – James Still

Contents

Acknowledgments

Every photographer needs co-laborers. I am blessed to have one in my friend Al Fritsch. After two books and 20 calendars for ASPI (Appalachia-Science in the Public Interest) we decided it was time to renew our partnership — hence this book.

Also special thanks to Mark Spencer for the many trips together searching out places to photograph for ASPI. I could not have done it without the help and influence of my wife Pat, my children, Scharme who created the original design and layout, Gwen, for patient technical support and Kara Beth, for advice and use of studio space. Thanks also to our four artistic grandchildren, as well as the tolerant employees of Brunner Studio. All had a hand in the production of this book.

Thanks to the many people of Appalachia who opened the doors of their homes and lives to me. They have given me directions when I was lost, helped me change flat tires, pulled me out of mud holes and creeks, shared stories of interesting people and places, fed me, and opened their hearts to this camera-man with the Wisconsin accent.

A special thanks goes out to Al's brother, Frank and his sister, Pat. This book would have been impossible without their help.

These photographs were taken over a 50-year span. Many convey a culture and way of life that is passing, moments gone forever. Yet, conjoined, the mountains and people remain. Al and I hope that through the photos and meditations the readers/viewers will see the handiwork of God.

Invitation

The Appalachian Mountains influence us in many ways and, in their own way, help raise our hearts and minds to God. Also they are able to change the way we live and think about ourselves and others. Mountains have their own characteristics and when we live among them; these good attributes help make us better for being here. This interaction of land and people is worth reflecting upon and we are convinced is worth passing on to others.

We seek to demonstrate the ABCs of just some of these mountain characteristics through photographs and accompanying reflections and prayers. We suspect that we have only tapped the surface and that deep within the recesses of our hills are many other wonderful characteristics that are awaiting discovery. Our invitation is that you attend to the mountain moments of your own lives and help us uncover the spiritual wealth that is forthcoming. We would like to know your own thinking on this subject.

Warren Brunner

Al Fritsch, SJ

Awe

Before the mountains
were settled,
before the hills,
I came to birth;
before God made
the earth,
the countryside,
or the first grains
of the world's dust.
(Proverbs 8:25-26)

Reflection

$\mathcal{W}$e are present in the Creator's mind and heart, even before these ancient mountains formed from the drifting continents, the ripples of Pangea's wanderings. We are part of the womb of Earth herself and are bonded to these hills. Thus we start to realize our kinship by being Appalachian to the core. Yes, we are struck with a sense of awe, that mixture of reverence, wonder and fear, with God's presence rendering the first, our mountains the second, and our own inadequateness before such Mystery the third. In awe we find our place, we know our presence, and we have the energy to move forward ever so gently into the future that draws us forth.

Moments of Wonder

Prayer

Transcendent God, give us the gentle step that it takes to walk with a light footprint and never hurt the fragile mother that is our Earth. Help us to move forward with a steady step.

Direction

Reflection

*W*e are prone to get lost without landmarks and need help in finding our way. Hills and coves and creeks can be confusing, and thus we need prominent landmarks of various types. Mountains can stand out as pointers showing the right direction. But people on the way need more: we need God's guiding hand to give us our orientation, our ultimate bearing.

From north, sharp winds of winter won
   can strike us when we try to run;
from east, rises the spring-found sun,
   reminding Earth that cold is gone;
from south, the summer's heat has spun
   to test the road that we are on;
and autumn's bright west-setting sun
   shows our journey has just begun.

*I lift up my eyes to
the mountains:
where is help to
come from?
(Psalm 121:1)*

Prayer

Omnipresent God, assist us who struggle on the way, to keep our bearing by means of the road markers of life, many of which we so easily overlook. Let our hills be our companions on our journey.

Expectancy

*Mountains of Israel, you
will grow branches
and bear fruit for
my people of
Israel, who will
soon return.
Yes I am coming to
you, I have turned to
you; you will be
tilled and sown.
(Ezekiel 36:8-9)*

Reflection

Mountaintops point heavenward and these, well-worn by maturity, give a promise of better things to come. Flowers, bright and pale, of various shades and hues, appear upon their heights amid rocks and windswept crevices. These give special color to the landscape, a promise of something new that awaits a better season. Although birds come and go, northward or southward, a number have determined to stay, for they know no special travel season; the cardinal, wren, crow and jay give us the hope that spring opens into an eternal day. With more or less permanently folded hands, the mountains and their plants and animals turn our gaze heavenward as we await in breathless expectancy the better times ahead.

Prayer

Emmanuel, give us the sense of hopeful waiting that something better is in store for us. Let the mountains indicate through ever-refreshing cover; let them help us communicate this sense of promise to others.

Humility

Reflection

M ountains have strengths and weaknesses. High places mean power and haughty might, but those seeking such places will be brought low on the Day of the Lord. The Appalachian range is hardly lofty by younger mountain standards (Rockies, Himalayas, and Andes), since at best this range reaches a mile above sea level. Being older and wiser, the Appalachians teach us that all creatures need to bow low before the majesty of God. The irony is that in doing so, one receives a more elevated state for, through humility, we discover our true worth. Note that we speak in spiritual terms, for we do not advocate mountain top removal nor the physical cutting of each of us down to a legless state. In finding our true condition we also find our true elevated state, for ultimately humility breeds honesty, and in truth rests justice for all.

Let every valley be
filled in,
every mountain and
hill be laid low,
let every cliff become
a plain,
and the ridges a
valley;...
(Isaiah 40:4; also
Luke 3:4-6)

Prayer

All powerful Lord of all, help us to discover who we truly are, and in doing so help expose our false airs; help us to join others and through humble service to bring about your kingdom.

Kindness

Reflection

*A*ll too often our journey is tiresome, the weather is bitter, the land seems gloomy; certain times and seasons wear on us. But wait a moment! Depression must not ruin our lives. Kindness is all about, and we are led by the Lord at all times. Look more deeply! The dewdrops and snow crystals gleam in the early morning sun; in the angle we observe them we discover the spectrum of light turned into rubies, sapphires, emeralds, topazes. These bejewel our landscape, the early sequins that kiss our land ever so briefly; they are precious moments that soon depart but show ever so vividly the kindness of our God. The sun warms, the drops evaporate, our concerns crowd out such moments, but should they? God's kindness remains and always brings us comfort.

Though I pass through a gloomy valley,
I fear no harm;
beside me your rod and your staff
are there to hearten me.
(Psalm 23:4)

Prayer

Good Shepherd, show us your kindness even when we only see the gloom and never the brightness of your light. Help us resolve to record precious moments so as to help brighten the gloomy who seek to leave their valley for the heights of lights.

Neighborliness

Helping Moments

How good, how
   delightful it is for
   all to live together
   like brothers:

Copious as a Hermon
   dew falling on the
   heights of Zion,
   where YHWH
   confers his
   blessing,
   everlasting life.
   (Psalm 133:1,3)

Reflection

*O*ur mountains stand as our sisters and brothers, our neighbors, sharing with us who live here the hard times we experience. Plains people sometimes visit and sometimes voice a word, claustrophobia, when surrounded by highlands. Those of us who scratch here for a living get in closer touch with the neighborhood. We know that the mountains guard us against the biting winds of winter and angry storms as well; they allow the mists to hang over the valleys and provide cool shade in summer; they give us scenic views of fresh buds, green foliage, and colored leaves to soothe our nerves. Mountains teach us to see others as kin or good as kin. We invite those from far-off places to come and celebrate with us, and we settle old feuds in friendly ways.

Prayer

Holy God, allow us to grow in our bonds with others and to be willing to see mountains not as barriers but rather as the inviting hands that go out to all the world.

Thankfulness

Moments of Gratitude

Reflection

*I*n all seasons we give thanks for all people in our lives and many, many other things as well:

January – cozy fires, preserved food, greenhouse greens;
February – strengthening sun, seedling starts;
March – strong winds, fresh dandelions, peeping
       crocus buds;
April – showers, jumping fish, passing birds, poke shoots;
May – many wildflowers, tree foliage, peas, strawberries;
June – raspberries, chard, onions, lettuce, cherries;
July – plums, cucumbers, peaches, new potatoes,
       new-mown hay;
August – tomatoes, sweet corn, beans, apricots, fireflies;
September – goldenrod, ironweed, apples, grapes; peppers;
October – pears, squirrel, squash, fall greens, persimmons;
November – pumpkin pie, turkey, cranberry, popcorn, turnips;
December – hickory nuts, horseradish, Christmas delights.

When that day comes,
*   the mountains will run*
*   with new wine*
*   and the hills flow with*
*   milk,*
*   and all the river beds of*
*   Judah*
*   will run with water.*
*   (Joel 4:18a)*

Prayer

Generous God, receive our gratitude at this moment for all things, those named and those we so often forget. Help us spread a spirit of thanksgiving to all we meet.

Witness

Reflection

The mountains stand as silent witnesses to the movements all about, especially the misdeeds among and to them. The Creator honors the highlands to store up the experience of ages. They are sensitive to tragedies that have befallen them through disrespectful visitors and this is manifested by the inability of some human beings to form perfect community there. Do stones speak out?

We too are called to be witnesses and must learn from the mountains. We experience wrongdoing as well and must listen, gather information, monitor the happenings, and speak out to the proper authorities. We cannot remain silent for we have voices and a sense of responsibility. At times we must act for we are witnesses to the mountains themselves.

*Listen you mountains,
to YHWH's accusation,
give ear, you
foundations of the
earth.*
(Micah 6:2)

Prayer

Oh Lord, maker of all good things, make us caring people who see mischief when it occurs, and are willing to take corrective measures.

138